Deep

Indust

Advisory

Committee

. . . .

Guidance on the design, installation and use of free standing support systems (including powered supports) in coal mines

HSE BOOKS

This guidance was prepared, in consultation with the
Health and Safety Executive (HSE), by a working group
representative of all sides of the deep coal mining
industry. The guidance represents what members of the
working group consider to be good practice. It has been
agreed by the Deep Mined Coal Industry Advisory
Committee and the Health and Safety Commission.

Following the guidance is not compulsory and you are
free to take other action. But if you do follow the
guidance you will normally be doing enough to comply
with the law. Health and safety inspectors seek to secure
compliance with the law and may refer to this guidance
as illustrating good practice.

. . . .

CONTENTS

. . . .

WHO SHOULD READ THIS BOOKLET?

1   This guidance sets out the key elements for the safe use of free standing support systems. It is one of a series providing guidance on the design of ground control measures and their safe application and use below ground in coal mines. It is aimed at:

■   owners;

■   managers;

■   other people, including members of the management structure, whose duties include the assessment, design, supervision or monitoring of free standing support systems;

■   people whose duties include the installation or withdrawal of free standing supports;

■   safety representatives.

2   Many of the principles in this guidance are also relevant to those non-coal mines that use free standing support systems to control ground movement.

WHAT ARE FREE STANDING SUPPORT SYSTEMS?

3   In coal mines, the strata is generally not strong enough to support itself and ground control measures are needed, in the form of either free standing support systems or reinforcement systems, or both. In such circumstances effective ground control measures should ensure that the newly exposed roof and, where necessary, the sides, are secured systematically, quickly, effectively and safely.

4   Free standing support systems should keep the roof and sides of underground working places and roadways secure so they can be used safely for as long as they are needed. They include:

■   props, bars, arches or chocks;

■   hydraulic props;

■   powered roof supports;

■   packing or stowing of excavated areas.

5   A glossary of terms used in this booklet can be found at the end.

6   Further guidance on the application of ground reinforcement techniques in coal mines can be found in the relevant Deep Mined Coal Industry Advisory

Committee publications listed in the references in Appendix 3 at the end of this booklet. However, in this booklet, the sections on:

■ assessment;

■ design; and

■ ground control rules

are relevant to all types of ground control measures, including those that rely on strata reinforcement rather than free standing support.

THE LEGAL FRAMEWORK

7   This booklet includes within the text a number of references to relevant legislation. Unless otherwise stated, these references are to the **Mines (Control of Ground Movement) Regulations 1999** and its associated Approved Code of Practice (ACOP). Following this guidance means that people will normally be doing enough to comply with the law, but they should still familiarise themselves with their legal duties under the Regulations, and with the ACOP, which gives practical advice on how to comply with them.

8   The above Regulations are made under the **Health and Safety at Work etc Act 1974**, which applies to all employers, employees and self-employed people. The Act protects not only people at work but also members of the public who may be affected by work activity. Appendix 2 contains further guidance on application of health and safety law to the self-employed.

The Mines (Control of Ground Movement) Regulations 1999

9   Regulation 4 requires managers to ensure that the ground control measures in use at their mines will keep secure those places where people work or pass. To help managers achieve this, the Regulations require them to follow a four-stage process to assess - design - implement - audit and review. Specifically, the Regulations include the following provisions relating to the assessment of ground conditions and to the design, installation and monitoring of ground control measures:

■ **Stage 1 (regulation 5)** - requires the assessment of ground conditions before starting any excavation. The purpose of the assessment is to provide information about the area of the mine to be excavated, and to help determine what measures should be taken to control ground movement, including the type of free standing support system appropriate to the circumstances.

■ **Stage 2 (regulation 6)** - covers the design of the support system, taking into account the findings of the Stage 1 assessment. In relation to free standing support systems the design should set out the measures necessary to effectively control the roof, sides and face;

. . . .

- **Stage 3 (regulation 7)** - requires managers to make rules to implement the design. These will provide the information and instructions needed by those who are to install the support system.

- **Stage 4 (regulation 10)** - requires managers to assess the adequacy of ground control measures - in this case, free standing support systems. In other words, to put in place monitoring systems and, based on the results from these, to audit and review how the ground control measures are performing.

10 Each stage acts as a check on the effectiveness of the previous stage, and opens up the whole process to continual review.

11 Managers can undertake these duties themselves if they are competent to do so. However, they can appoint one or more suitably qualified and competent people to do it on their behalf.

12 In certain circumstances managers will need to notify the Health and Safety Executive (HSE) of what they intend to do at least 28 days before commencing work in that place. The Regulations also place duties on mine officials and workers in relation to the implementation of the rules, and the installation, withdrawal and replacement of support materials. Mine officials must also take steps to secure areas where falls have occurred.

13 This booklet includes more detailed guidance on all of these issues. Managers of small mines will find more guidance in HSE's *Ground control at small mines*, which is referenced at the end of this booklet.

Training **14** Everyone who is required to set or withdraw supports, or to supervise their setting or withdrawal, must be suitably trained and competent to do so. More details of the training requirements will be found in the ACOP to regulation 25 of the Management and Administration of Safety and Health at Mines Regulations 1993 (MASHAM).

STAGE 1 - ASSESSING GROUND CONDITIONS

When to make an assessment **15** Before excavation starts, managers must ensure that an assessment is made of all factors likely to affect the movement of ground in that part of the mine (regulation 5 (a)). The level of detail to be included in the assessment will depend on both:

- the complexity of the proposed free standing support system(s);

- the level of knowledge, experience and expertise in working with such systems.

16 In many cases, assessment will be a relatively straightforward process founded on existing knowledge of the mining conditions in a particular locality, seam or mine.

. . . .

17 Where there is a need to know accurately the properties of the coal seam and the strata above and below it, the process of assessment may be more detailed, for instance when:

■ new or significantly different techniques are used, such as sprayed linings or concrete segments;

■ rock bolts are used systematically as a supplementary means of controlling the movement of ground in roadways where free standing support is the principal means of ground control;

■ making the transition from free standing supports to a system relying principally on strata reinforcement by rock bolts (see reference in Appendix 3).

Steps of the
assessment

18 The steps to take to assess ground conditions are:

■ collecting relevant information;

■ assessing that information to identify what support arrangements might be appropriate to the circumstances;

■ recording the findings of the assessment;

■ deciding the area over which the assessment is considered valid.

Step 1 - Collecting the information

19 The type of information collected will include:

■ geological information, such as the type, thickness and condition of the rock beds adjacent to the proposed extraction, including any geological disturbances;

■ the properties of the coal seam and of the rocks above and below the seam;

■ the findings of any site investigation relevant to the area to be worked, including whether or not water is present and, if so, its likely effect;

■ previous experience;

■ relevant historical data.

20 Information on the type of strata above and below the excavation may be determined from:

■ site investigations carried out in existing roadways in the vicinity of the proposed workings;

■ knowledge and experience of ground conditions from comparable workings

■ old mine plans;

■ exploratory borehole records;

■ examination of the strata at either side of any exposed geological fault.

Figure 1: Looking at the condition of existing roadways is one way of collecting information. In this case, the arch supports are standing well, but lateral stress is causing floor heave

21 Detailed site investigation may be necessary where:

■ workings are proposed in a new seam or a new area of a seam;

■ there is reason to suspect that there may be a material change in the nature of the strata or general mining conditions.

Step 2 - Assessing the information

22 Once sufficient information has been collected, managers should assess it, or make sure that some suitably competent person assesses it on their behalf. The assessment should take into account as appropriate:

■ the likely effects of vertical and lateral stresses, including those that are likely to be caused by mineral extraction in the same or other seams;

■ the effect of surface features, such as rapidly increasing or reducing cover in hilly areas;

■ the magnitude and nature of expected ground movement;

■ the potential for support system failure;

■ the possible effects from, and on, other working places.

Step 3 - Recording the findings

23 When the assessment has been completed, it should be summarised in a document (regulation 5(b)) containing:

■ the assessment procedure, including, where relevant, details of the type and nature of any site investigation;

■ assumptions made;

■ significant findings;

■ conclusions.

24 For most free standing support systems, the assessment document can be both simple and brief.

Step 4 - Deciding the area over which the assessment is valid

25 The area of the mine for which a particular assessment can be considered valid will depend on the amount and quality of information available at the time the assessment is made.

26 Where a seam is being worked for the first time, information on the type and nature of the strata and general mining conditions will be limited. Therefore it may not be possible to assess confidently what the ground conditions will be like across the whole of the area to be worked. An assessment made in these circumstances should only be relied on during the early stages of excavation.

27 As work progresses and more information is collected, managers should periodically review the assessment. If the behaviour of the ground can be predicted with confidence over a wider area, managers can then extend the area for which the assessment is valid.

Further assessment **28** Managers must ensure that they make a further assessment:

■ if they suspect that there has been a material change in conditions since the initial assessment;
■ to enable the assessment to be brought up-to-date as more information becomes available in the course of working the mine (see regulation 5(c)).

Material changes **29** A material change is a change in ground conditions, not anticipated at the time of the assessment and therefore not covered by it, which might lead to a change in the system of support.

30 Managers should be able to recognise material changes. If they are in any doubt whether something is a material change, they should treat it as one. For example, a material change might be where mine workings move into an area where the ground is much weaker than expected. In such circumstances, managers would need to:

■ collect the available information on the weaker ground, perhaps by inspecting the site;

■ reassess the ground conditions;

■ review, and if necessary, revise the assessment and design documents;

■ implement any changes to the free standing support system made necessary by the change in ground conditions.

31 In this particular example, it is likely that managers would:

■ note the weak ground in their assessment of ground conditions;

■ conclude that the roadway supports needed to be more closely spaced for the extent of the weak ground;

■ reflect the changes to the support system in both the design document and support rules relating to that place, and to any other place likely to be affected by the same material change.

32 If a change proposed in the design of the support system is a significant change within the meaning of the Regulations, managers must notify HSE (see regulation 8). You will find more guidance on significant changes and on notifying HSE later in this booklet.

STAGE 2 - PREPARING THE DESIGN

33 Four basic principles apply to the design of free standing support systems:

■ they have to be strong enough to control ground movement adequately;

■ they have to be capable of being implemented safely;

■ the amount of ground exposed during each operational cycle should be kept to the practical minimum, considering the method of work and the proposed support system;

■ appropriate temporary support or reinforcement should be used at various stages in the support setting cycle; for example, temporary props, forepoles (horseheads) or spot bolts.

34 Once the assessment has been completed and recorded, managers must ensure that a design is prepared setting out the measures necessary to control ground movement in the area to be worked. The design may comprise both text and illustrations. Those preparing the design should take account of any significant findings arising out of the initial assessment of ground conditions (see regulation 6(1)(a)). For example, if the assessment has identified an area of weak ground, then support spacing might need to be reduced and/or a stronger type of support used in that area.

35 The design should include a description of the proposed support system. It should also include information on potential hazards so that managers can take account of them in devising a safe method of work.

36 The design should include as appropriate:

■ excavation dimensions, for example the roadway size or face layout;

■ the limits of extraction;

■ minimum pillar sizes;

■ the support density, for example spacing between adjacent supports;

■ details of any material or equipment forming part of any ground control system, including, if appropriate, any specifications;

■ the proposed method of work;

■ procedures for dealing with abnormalities;

■ information on other hazards, such as known zones of weakness, proximity to other workings, or boreholes.

37 There are some minimum legal requirements for the spacing or density of support, which have been determined after years of experience in a wide range of conditions. These are set out in the Schedule to regulation 8(3) of the Mines (Control of Ground Movement) Regulations 1999. This Schedule is reproduced in Appendix 1 of this booklet.

38 Where an existing design has already been proved, it may be used in other places, provided managers have taken steps to ascertain that the ground conditions at these sites are similar to those where the design has already been proved.

Reviewing and revising the design

39 The design will need to be reviewed and, if necessary, revised if there are material changes in the assessment or changes to the working methods (see regulation 6(1)(b)).

STAGE 3 - IMPLEMENTING THE DESIGN

Preparing manager's support rules

40   The law requires managers to ensure the preparation of suitable and sufficient rules that set out the ground control measures to be taken, and how to implement them (see regulation 7(1)(a)). The generic name 'manager's support rules', or just 'support rules', tends to be used whatever type of ground control measures they refer to - free standing support, reinforcement by rock bolts, or a combination of the two.

41   To be suitable manager's support rules need to be fit for the purpose for which they are designed. To be sufficient they must contain enough information to describe:

■   the relevant ground control measures, by reference to the design;

■   the step-by-step procedure that mine workers should follow to safely implement the measures.

42   The rules should therefore:

■   include simple drawings, diagrams or photographs;

■   explain what is required at each stage of the support-setting operations.

43   Drawings or diagrams that show only the end result, for example the arrangement of steel work at a junction, are neither suitable nor sufficient as support rules.

Where are rules needed?

44   Rules are needed for every place in a mine where ground is being excavated or exposed, including:

■   coal faces;

■   faces being prepared for salvage, or faces being salvaged;

■   headings;

■   junctions;

■   engine houses;

■   refuge holes;

■   shafts and staple shafts;

■   horizontal and vertical bunkers;

■   rippings and back rippings;

- excavations made to facilitate the installation, maintenance, repair etc of plant and equipment; for example, changing drums on coal face cutting machines.

45   In addition, where a roadway is to break through (thirl) into an existing roadway, appropriate support arrangements, which may include an increase in support density, should be made and included in the rules.

46   The roadway into which the new road will thirl will probably require extra support or reinforcement to secure its stability at the point of breakthrough, and from 5 m to 20 m on either side, depending on conditions. For example, it may be necessary to set a row of wooden chocks close to the rib side to control the loose edge where the new roadway is planned to thirl. In such circumstances, managers need to draw up new rules that clearly set out where and how the extra support or reinforcement is to be installed.

47   One set of rules may apply to more than one working place, provided that the working methods at those places are comparable. In this event, the rules should make clear:

- to which working places they apply;

- the date they became effective.

What should support rules do?

48   The rules should explain the ground control measures that need to be taken in the part(s) of the mine to which they apply.

49   They should set out the method of work to be followed to minimise the risks from falls of ground, and from setting or withdrawing a free standing support system. In particular, they should:

- show the stage-by-stage sequence of support operations;

- show the layout and dimensions of the free standing support system;

- restrict to a practical minimum the amount of ground exposed during each operational cycle, taking into account the system of work;

- provide for everyone, including the driver or operator of any machine, to be at a safe distance from the unsupported face, roof or sides to prevent injury from any fall which may occur in advance of the last support;

- specify other preventive and protective measures (for example, the use of forepoles, drop-arms and side shields) at appropriate points in the excavation and setting cycle.

Drawing up support rules

50   The experience of the officials and workers who will have to implement the support rules will be helpful in drawing up the rules, and the manager should seek their views on the form, content and practicability of the rules.

51 Support rules should incorporate requirements for safe methods of work. These will be based on risk assessments carried out in accordance with the requirements of regulation 3 of the Management of Health and Safety at Work Regulations 1999.

52 For most coal measures strata, the likelihood of a fall from unsupported roof, face or sides is high. Therefore, in drawing up a safe method of work, managers should consider:

■ the length of time workers have to spend close to open ground from which a fall might occur;

■ the likelihood that falling ground might strike a worker;

■ the consequences of that happening.

53 Associated risks should also be taken into account, such as handling or operating supports and machinery (for example, the movement of a road header during whole-arch setting operations).

54 Other factors may be relevant, including:

■ the maintenance of ventilation;

■ the safe operation of transport systems;

■ service requirements.

Making the rules clear

55 The law requires managers to make sure that people understand the rules that are relevant to them (see regulation 7(2)). Officials and workers also have legal duties to implement the rules and therefore, managers need to prepare them in a form that can be readily and easily understood. They should consider showing a draft of the rules to officials, workers who will have to implement them, and safety representatives, to check that the rules are clear and that they can understand them.

What should be in the rules?

56 Paragraph 31 of the Approved Code of Practice sets out minimum requirements for the content of rules. This booklet repeats these below for convenience:

Extract from the Approved Code of Practice, paragraph 31

57 At all mines where ground control measures include the use of support materials, the rules should include, as appropriate, details of:

(a) the method of work;

(b) the support materials and equipment to be used;

(c)   the support density;

(d)   the layout and dimensions of any system of support designed to control the movement of ground, including where appropriate the maximum distance(s) between:

   (i)   adjacent powered support centres;

   (ii)   the roof beam tip of any powered roof support and the face;

   (iii)   the front row of props and the face;

   (iv)   adjacent props;

   (v)   adjacent bars;

   (vi)   adjacent arches or other free standing roadway support;

   (vii) adjacent rock bolts (note - this applies where rock bolts are used systematically as a supplementary means of support);

   (viii) subsequent support setting cycles;

   (ix)   the last row of rock bolts or the last free standing support and the face at its furthest point; and

   (x)   the front of the pack or packs and the face.

(e)   any method of temporary support necessary to secure safety;
   [notes - for free standing supports this would include details of temporary support procedures, including:

   -      the procedure for providing ground reinforcement or support to the face and exposed roof where mineworkers are required to work on the face side of the AFC spill plates;

   -      exposed ground where mining machinery cannot be withdrawn from the face of the heading for repair]

(f)   the procedures for dealing with abnormal situations (such as a fall or cavity);

(g)   the method and equipment for withdrawal of support (see also regulation 13 and paragraph 46 of the ACOP);

(h)   any monitoring arrangements for confirming that the support system continues to be effective.

58   The key measurements should be clearly shown, including details of temporary support (see Schedule to regulation 8(3) in Appendix 1).

59   The rules should also make it clear that support materials additional to those specified in the rules can be installed, if necessary, to secure safety.

· ·

Page 12 Deep Mined Coal Industry Advisory Committee

Signing the rules

60 The manager should reference, sign and date each set of rules, so that people who have to implement the rules are clear about which ones are in force.

Making the rules more accessible

61 Support rules need to be readily accessible at all times to people who have to follow them. They may want to refer to them before going down the mine or at any time during the shift.

62 Copies of all sets of rules in force at a mine must be posted in the covered accommodation (see regulation 35 of the MASHAM Regulations 1993).

63 Copies of the rules, or relevant extracts from them, applying to a particular place (or places) should also be posted at the entrance to part(s) of a mine to which those rules apply. They should be posted in a position where they can easily be seen and read (see regulation 7(3)(a)).

64 Managers also have to ensure that the rules, or relevant extracts from them, are made available to all people in the mine whose duties include taking ground control measures, or who have the responsibility for ensuring such measures are taken (see regulation 7(3)(b)). To meet this requirement in practice, the rules, or relevant extracts of the rules, could either be:

■ posted sufficiently close to the place(s) to which they apply; or

■ issued to individual workers and officials.

Checking that the rules work in practice

65 Workers, who will have to comply with the rules, and officials, who will have to implement them, may have been consulted during the preparation of the rules. However, managers still need to ensure that the systems of work set out in the rules are achievable.

66 When the support system is first implemented, the manager or some other senior member of the management structure should spend some time with those at the working place to assess whether:

■ the free standing support system is adequate;

■ each stage in the cycle of operations can be safely achieved.

67 In order to do this, it will be necessary to look at what the workers do at each stage in the cycle of operations and assess the risks to them (see regulation 3 of the Management of Health and Safety at Work Regulations 1999 and associated ACOP paragraphs). Significant findings should be recorded. An example of a significant finding would be the need to change the support system, or the cycle of operations, to avoid, or further reduce, risks to those setting support.

Reviewing and revising the rules

68 If the design of the ground control measures is changed, or if the method of work is to be changed, then the rules will need to be reviewed and, if necessary, revised (see regulation 7(1)(b)).

69 Rules must be regularly reviewed to check that they are still relevant to the operations being carried on, and, if necessary, revised. The rules should also be reviewed, and if necessary revised, after:

■ any fall of ground accident;

■ any fall of ground, not a part of normal operations at a mine, which results from a significant failure of ground control measures;

■ anyone (whose duties include implementing the rules, or ensuring that the rules are implemented) informs the manager that the rules cannot be complied with.

STAGE 4 - ASSESSING THE ADEQUACY OF FREE STANDING SUPPORT SYSTEMS

Support systems monitoring

70 Underground support systems are often subject to ground stresses high enough to cause them to deteriorate over time. Supports can also corrode, causing them to weaken. Ground movement might displace them. It is therefore important that support systems at a mine are properly monitored.

71 The aim of monitoring support systems is to ensure that managers (and others in the management structure who might need it) have enough information to assess the adequacy of free standing support systems. In this way they can identify potential problems and take steps to deal with them.

The manager's assessment scheme

72 Under regulation 10(a), managers have a duty to make sure that an appropriate scheme is in place for assessing the adequacy of ground control measures. Paragraphs 39-43 of the ACOP and guidance explain the purpose of the scheme, which type(s) of monitoring may be suitable, and what should be done with the results. The type(s), frequency and extent of monitoring set out in the scheme will depend on the ground conditions and the support systems in use.

73 It is important that the monitoring procedures set out in the scheme are such that any defect or abnormality that gives rise (or is likely to give rise to) increased risks, is brought quickly to the attention of those who can take steps to rectify it.

74 The scheme should be suitable for the circumstances in which it is to be applied. It should clearly set out:

■ who does what in terms of monitoring the condition of support systems;

■ how monitoring information is recorded;

■ who should act on the information.

Collecting the information

75 For those systems that use 'traditional' methods of support such as props and bars or arches, a suitable monitoring scheme might rely wholly on the collection of information obtained from inspections made by district officials under regulation 12 of the MASHAM Regulations 1993.

76 Where other means of collecting information are in place, for example, monitoring by ground control specialists, managers may still want to use district officials to monitor the condition of support systems through inspection, and to use their statutory reports as a means of collecting more information.

Figure 2: Official inspecting the condition of supports in an arched roadway

77 Where inspection officials and their reports form part of the monitoring arrangements, managers should ensure that the officials' reports include sufficient detail on:

■ the state of the roof and sides;

■ the condition of the support systems,

to enable the manager to assess the adequacy of the support systems, or for someone else to assess it on the manager's behalf.

Making assessments

78 The information collected should be used to assess the adequacy of support systems. The manager or whoever makes the assessment will need to take into account:

■ the nature of the ground controlled by the support system;

■ the likelihood of failure in the strata or support system;

■ any measuring or monitoring trends.

· ·

(b)   from one rockbolting system to another not used at the mine before;

(c)   from rock bolts to any free standing support system not used at the mine before;

(d)   from any free standing support system to a rock bolt system not used at the mine before;

(e)   from props and bars to powered supports;

(f)   from powered supports to props and bars;

(g)   in the design of bord and pillar workings;

(h)   where, although the proposed system has been used previously at the mine, the current management team has no experience of its use at the mine.

SETTING AND WITHDRAWING SUPPORTS

92   The installation, withdrawal or disturbance of supports is one of the higher risk operations carried out at coal mines. It is important that this work is properly organised and controlled so that it is carried out in line with the manager's support rules.

The role of mine officials

93   In order to carry out their duties effectively, officials should familiarise themselves with support rules.

94   Officials must take all reasonable steps to ensure that support rules are implemented (see regulation 19(a)). Officials should periodically discuss the requirements of the rules with the people in their charge, and test their understanding of them.

95   When checking that workers are setting support safely and in accordance with the rules, officials should check:

■   the roof and sides for signs of any weakness;

■   that the support system (including any temporary support) is set properly;

■   what those setting support are doing at each stage in the cycle of operations;

■   the availability of support materials.

96   Before leaving the working place, officials should give workers instructions for safe working.

97   If an official finds it difficult to implement any of the support rules, he should take steps to ensure that the manager is made aware of such difficulties.

· ·

The role of workers

98 People installing, withdrawing or disturbing supports also have legal duties to comply with the rules that apply (see regulation 12(1)).

Excavating the ground

99 Support rules for drivages will include:

- the maximum distance permitted from the last completed support to the newly excavated face;

- the maximum advance per cycle.

100 Although these distances should never be exceeded, the amount of ground excavated at any one time should not exceed the minimum required to enable the next support setting cycle to be completed. This might be less than the amount specified in support rules, particularly if supports are being set at smaller intervals than the maximum permitted by support rules.

Setting supports

101 Once enough ground has been excavated, workers must start to set support immediately (see regulation 5(1) of the MASHAM Regulations). The longer the ground is left unsupported, the more unstable it becomes and a fall of ground is more likely. This increases the risks to people who will have to set support.

102 If supports cannot be set immediately after excavation, for whatever reason, workers must:

- withdraw to a place of safety;

- prevent access to the exposed area;

- tell an official (see regulation 12(2)(a)).

103 Similarly, if any supports seem to have become unstable or unsuitable, workers must:

- make that support stable; or

- replace it.

104 To make a support stable, it may be necessary to set additional supports alongside, or close to, the unsuitable or unstable support.

105 If a support can neither be made stable nor replaced, and additional support cannot be set, workers must:

- immediately withdraw to a place of safety;

- prevent access to the place where the support has become unstable or unsuitable;

■ report the condition of the support to an official (see regulation 12(3)(b)).

106 A place of safety will usually be under supports far enough from the exposed ground, so that if a fall of roof or sides occurs it could not strike anyone. The distance will depend on local circumstances; for instance, a greater distance may be required in steeply rising roadways, where falling material could roll, bounce or slide along the sloping floor.

107 Access to places where support cannot be set, or where unstable or unsuitable supports cannot be remedied, can be easily and quickly prevented either by:

■ posting a sentry or sentries; or

■ effectively fencing off the approach(es) to the exposed ground and, where necessary, posting a danger sign or signs.

108 If a mine official thinks there are not enough support materials, or receives a report from someone that supports cannot be installed, or that unstable or unsuitable support materials cannot be made stable or replaced, he must take steps to ensure that:

■ everyone is withdrawn to a place of safety;

■ access to the exposed ground is prevented;

■ the situation is remedied (regulations 11(4), 11(5) and 12(4)).

109 If the situation cannot be remedied before the end of the shift, the official must pass on information to his counterpart on the next working shift (regulation 10(5) of the MASHAM Regulations 1993). The information should enable his counterpart to:

■ decide what they have to do to remedy the situation;

■ instruct those under their command so that they can take appropriate action.

110 If anyone has withdrawn (or has been withdrawn) to a place of safety because of a lack of support materials, the official in charge of that part of the mine should ensure that no one returns or goes to that workplace until enough support materials are available for it to be properly supported.

Temporary support   **111** Everyone installing support should pay particular attention to the temporary support procedures specified in support rules.

Additional support   **112** Officials should ensure that additional support is set if they think it necessary (regulation 9(b)).

113 Extra support material to that required by the rules may be installed by anyone who has reason to believe that it is necessary in the interests of their own safety, or that of others (regulation 7(4)), and who is suitably trained and competent to set it (regulation 26 of the MASHAM Regulations 1993).

114 Anyone who is not suitably trained and competent to set support but has reason to believe that additional support is necessary to secure safety, should withdraw to a place of safety and notify an official (regulation 5(3) of the MASHAM Regulations 1993); for example, when somebody passing along a roadway sees that a support has been dislodged or broken and thinks that extra support might be needed to secure safety.

Dealing with falls of roof and sides

115 Falls of ground present particular risks to those working with support systems. Managers need to ensure that effective procedures are in place to minimise those risks that cannot be avoided. In particular, managers will need to ensure that only competent people experienced in that type of work carry it out.

116 In high-risk situations, managers should ensure that the work is closely supervised.

117 Manager's support rules should outline the method(s) of work to be adopted in the event of a fall of ground.

118 Workers should scale or dress loose material from the roof and sides. Wherever possible, they should do this from beneath permanent supports, using tools such as scaling bars. If they cannot carry out scaling from beneath permanent supports, then they should use temporary support, such as temporary props and bars, or protective equipment, such as forepoles, drop arms and side shields.

119 Managers' may need to put in place special procedures for dealing with large or awkward falls of ground, or where people may need to work in particularly hazardous areas, such as on the face side of AFC spill plates.

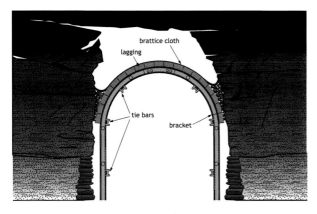

cross section

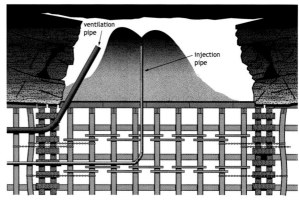

side section

Figure 3: Dealing with a large cavity in an existing roadway

Dealing with such falls can expose workers to high risks, so managers should ensure that this work is only carried out under the close supervision of competent officials. Support rules can only set out the general principles for supporting such falls and additional rules may be needed to deal with unusual circumstances.

120 Command supervisors are responsible for thoroughly supervising everyone working in the area of the mine for which they are responsible (regulation 10(2)(a) of the MASHAM Regulations 1993 and paragraphs 49-59 of the ACOP).

121 When there is a large or awkward fall, or when dealing with a fall in a particularly hazardous area, command supervisors should assess the situation and, as far as possible, remain at the fall area to closely supervise those dealing with the fall.

122 Command supervisors should not leave those dealing with falls of ground unless they cannot avoid it. For instance, a command supervisor may have to leave people dealing with one fall of ground to supervise people working on a second fall within their area of command. If so, before the command supervisor leaves, wherever possible he should summon another official to closely supervise those dealing with the first fall (MASHAM ACOP, paragraph 55).

123 If no other official is readily available, the command supervisor may instruct someone else in the procedure to be followed while he is away, provided they are competent (regulation 23 of the MASHAM Regulations 1993) and experienced in the type of work to be supervised (MASHAM ACOP, paragraph 60). In these circumstances, the command supervisor should return as soon as possible.

124 There may be abnormal situations, for example major falls, where a command supervisor has little experience of the type of work needed to recover

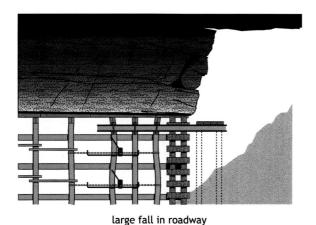

large fall in roadway

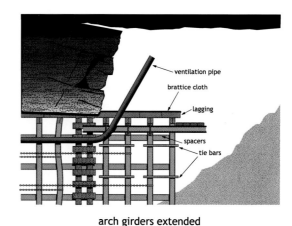

arch girders extended

Figure 4:

Dealing with a large cavity at the face of a heading

the fall. In such circumstances, the manager should take steps to ensure that a competent person who is experienced in such work is there to advise the command supervisor.

Installing support in emergencies

125 If a fall or unstable ground threatens the safety of anyone in the mine, support materials may be installed in a different way from that prescribed in the support rules so that people can withdraw to a place of safety.

Withdrawing support

126 Where supports are to be withdrawn, support rules should spell out the method(s) to be used. Anyone withdrawing support must:

■ use the safe method of work set out in the support rules;

■ do so only from a position of safety (regulation 13).

127 Some support operations involve temporarily withdrawing or disturbing supports; for example:

■ a hand-set hydraulic prop might be lowered in order to straighten it up or move it a short distance;

■ props in a roadway might be replaced individually without changing the bars.

128 The methods of work for temporarily withdrawing or disturbing supports need just as much planning as for total withdrawal. In particular, they should cater for temporary additional support to be installed before the permanent support is temporarily withdrawn or disturbed.

anchor prop

rope block

temporary prop

anchor prop

Figure 5:
Withdrawal of supports on a
prop and bar face

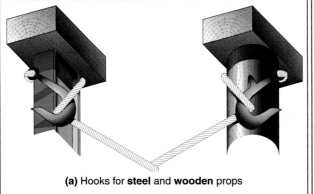

(a) Hooks for **steel** and **wooden** props

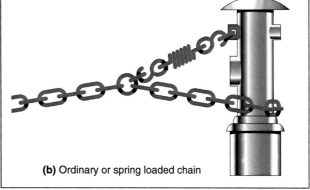

(b) Ordinary or spring loaded chain

Back ripping

129 Back ripping involves progressively withdrawing damaged and distorted supports, excavating ground to form a new profile and installing new supports. It is a potentially hazardous operation because the strata surrounding the damaged roadway has been deformed and weakened and is prone to falls of ground .

130 Back ripping should be planned and carried out to minimise the amount of exposed ground between old and new supports. The work should be thoroughly supervised by a command supervisor and should only be carried out by trained and experienced workers (back rippers).

131 The method of work for back ripping will be specified in manager's support rules. The method of work should specify:

■   how to withdraw supports safely;

■   what measures to take, including what additional support to set, to ensure that any fall in the back ripping area does not destabilise other roadway supports;

■   support-setting procedures, including temporary support measures;

■   what equipment to use;

■   how any equipment or services within the roadway are protected while back ripping is in progress.

132 Supports may be withdrawn safely from a distance by using a rope block, such as a tirfor. The attachments to anchor the blocks and to connect the rope to the support should be strong enough to withstand the expected load and should be fastened so that they do not slip.

133 Before a support is withdrawn, it should be adequately temporarily supported. One method of temporary support is to set one or more hydraulic props between the floor and the roof member of the support to be withdrawn. In very unstable roadways it may be necessary to install additional support before starting back ripping; for example, by setting wooden chocks and bars down the centre of the damaged roadway.

134 To prevent other supports falling uncontrollably when one support is withdrawn, at least four supports beyond the back ripping should be tied together; for example, by using tensioned chains.

135 Fishplates and struts should be removed before drawing off. These may be under stress and back rippers will need to take steps to ensure that the plates and struts do not violently spring out and cause injury when the fish bolts are removed. For fishplates, a long bolt should be inserted in place of the first fish bolt removed. This should give enough play to allow the fish plates to release when the remaining bolts are removed, but to stop them springing and causing injury. If struts are likely to spring violently, they can be restrained with a short safety chain before removing the strut bolts.

136 Where supports are very distorted and the fish bolts or struts cannot be removed manually, it may be necessary to crop them and remove the arches using powered equipment. This should only be done as part of a planned, closely supervised operation.

137 Once the support has been withdrawn and removed from the working area, support-setting operations should start. Temporary support should be set, or covering erected, to allow any further material to be removed safely from the roof - and, where arches are being set, from the shoulders - to allow the new permanent support roof member to be set and covered.

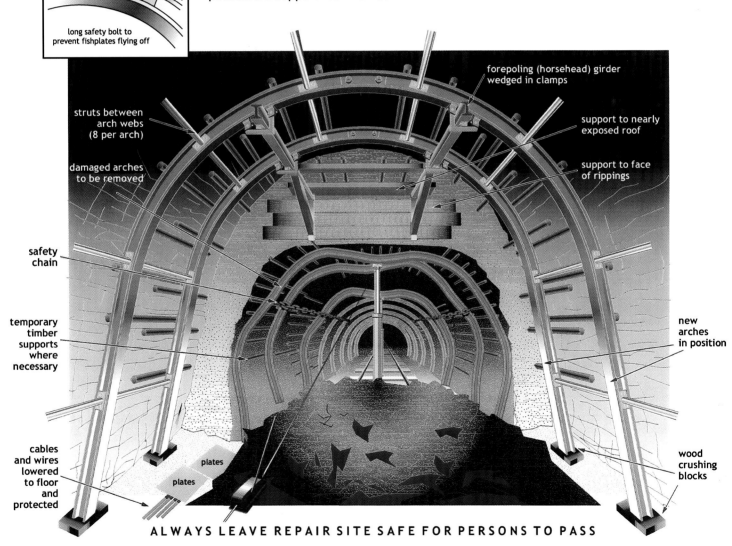

long safety bolt to prevent fishplates flying off

struts between arch webs (8 per arch)

damaged arches to be removed

safety chain

temporary timber supports where necessary

cables and wires lowered to floor and protected

plates

plates

forepoling (horsehead) girder wedged in clamps

support to nearly exposed roof

support to face of rippings

new arches in position

wood crushing blocks

ALWAYS LEAVE REPAIR SITE SAFE FOR PERSONS TO PASS

Figure 6: A typical layout of a back ripping in a badly distorted arch roadway

138 Horseheads, drop-arms and boards should temporarily support the exposed ripping face as soon as possible after workers have completed the temporary support necessary to protect themselves against falls from the roof and sides.

139 Any cavities above the new supports will need to be packed as soon as possible. This is one of the riskier stages of the support-setting operation and needs to be carefully planned. Where packing is to be inserted manually, it is best to cover the centre of the roof member first and place the packing material from beneath. The remaining covering can then be progressively installed and packed, working towards each side.

140 Temporary side support should be used, where necessary, to enable the sides to be flanked off so that the legs can be safely set, covered and packed.

141 Pump-packing several arches at once can significantly reduce the time people have to spend close to exposed ground and should be considered as an alternative to manual packing. However, it will still be necessary to place a layer of packing bags or fibre blocks behind the covering sheets to protect people against falls until the packing material can be pumped in.

142 Newly installed supports should be spaced at the same intervals as the ones being withdrawn or, where a manager wishes to set more support to reduce the chance of further deterioration, at reduced intervals.

143 It is advisable to have available several sets of struts of non-standard lengths to allow the position of the new supports to be adjusted if necessary, to keep the amount of exposed ground to a minimum.

144 In a roadway under repair, any equipment and services that cannot be removed need to be adequately protected. Pipe ranges should be lowered to

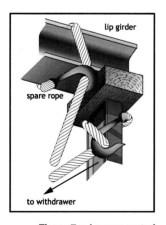

Figure 7a: Arrangement of ropes to withdraw a prop and bar

Figure 7b: Ripping the roadhead of a semi-mechanised face - lip girder about to be withdrawn

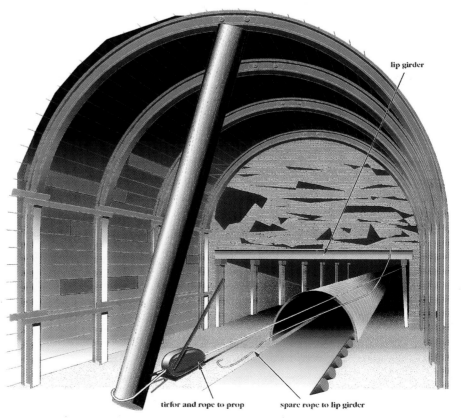

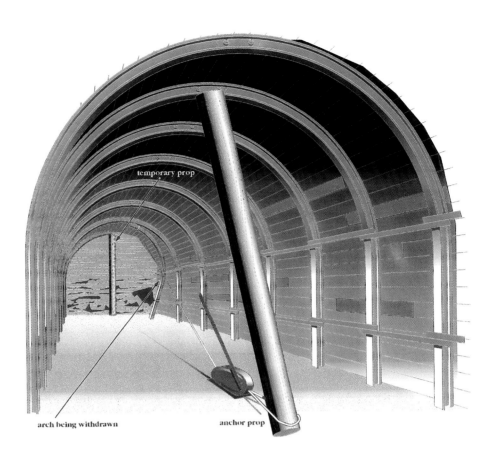

Figure 7c: *Drawing off in an abandoned roadway*

the floor and covered over. Power and communications cables should also be lowered to the floor and appropriately protected to prevent them being damaged by falling debris.

SUPPORT MATERIALS

Supply of support materials

145 Mine owners must make financial and other arrangements to ensure that a sufficient supply of suitable support materials is always available (regulation 11(1) and regulation 6(2) of the MASHAM Regulations 1993).

146 Workers at a mine should only install materials provided by the owner (regulation 11(1)).

147 Managers must ensure that enough support materials are available on site or close by when needed (regulation 11(2)). To comply with this, managers are advised to put procedures in place to ensure that people do not start to excavate the ground unless sufficient materials are already there to support the newly excavated ground.

148 Support materials will be suitable if they:

■ have previously been approved under the Coal and Other Mines (Support) Regulations 1966; or

- can be shown, by means of independently conducted and assessed type testing, to meet the criteria set out in a relevant British or European standard (see References at the end of this booklet); or

- have an acceptance number under the former British Coal Corporation's procedures for acceptance; or

- have been through a properly documented mine owner's acceptance procedure; and

- have, over a period of time, proved suitable for use in similar conditions.

149 Support materials not covered by these conditions, excluding wood, will be suitable if:

- they have been subjected to a test programme designed to simulate, as closely as is possible, operational conditions; and

- tests under this programme are conducted by an independent test house and a report is prepared; and

- an assessment of any risk to safety or health, or both, has been carried out; and

- the supplier of the product has a letter from the assessing body setting out the conditions under which the product may be used underground.

150 Some support materials, such as powered supports, will be 'work equipment' for the purposes of the Provision and Use of Work Equipment Regulations 1998. Mine owners and managers need to ensure that they comply with the relevant provisions of these Regulations.

151 Some support materials, again such as powered supports, will also be 'relevant machinery' for the purposes of the Supply of Machinery (Safety) Regulations 1992 and for the purposes of the Equipment and Protective Systems Intended for Use in Potentially Explosive Atmospheres Regulations 1996.

Prop and bar systems
152 Prop and bar systems are still used as a system of support in places including:

- hand-worked or partially-mechanised faces;

- face ends and roadheads on fully-mechanised faces;

- roadways;

- other locations for temporary support purposes.

153 Where props and bars are used on coal faces, the props should be set as close to the face as possible taking account of the system of work .

154 Two or more props should support each bar.

155 The number of props set under each bar should be sufficient to maintain the required support density over the width of the face working.

156 Hydraulic props and steel bars should be used in any place where an armoured face conveyor is in use and where the system of support involves advancing the props and bars during each cycle of operations.

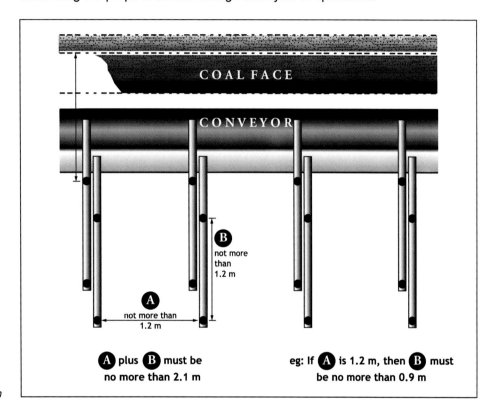

Figure 8: Twin bar system

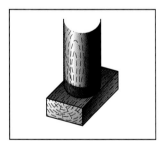

Figure 9: Wooden foot block under wood prop

157 Anyone setting a prop anywhere in a mine must set it securely and on a proper foundation. When the floor is soft, a prop may have to be set on a foot block or on a hard bed below the floor of the seam. Foot blocks should be at least twice the cross-sectional area of the prop on which they are set. A prop should not overlap any edge of the foot block under which it is set.

158 Wood props should be of good quality wood and have a reasonably consistent cross section. The prop diameter chosen will depend on both the height of the working and the anticipated load but should not be less than 75 mm. In workings where the extracted height exceeds 0.6 m, props should be a minimum 100 mm in diameter, and a minimum of 150 mm where the extracted height exceeds 1.8 m. Only props with a circular cross-section should be used for support on coal faces.

159 Wood props are sometimes used where the roof above the seam consists of relatively massive rocks that do not cave easily. Left in behind the face, they can help to control the rate of lowering of the roof beds above the goaf and limit the loads on coal face supports.

160 In most circumstances, wood props are not suitable on coal faces where the system of work is such that they would have to be advanced during each cycle. The props are not sufficiently robust and can tighten, causing difficulties when they have to be withdrawn. In extreme conditions they can violently spring out.

161 Hydraulic props provide a robust and flexible means of support. They can be set tightly to the roof anywhere within their working range. If necessary, they can be withdrawn remotely by attaching a chain, wire or rope to their valves.

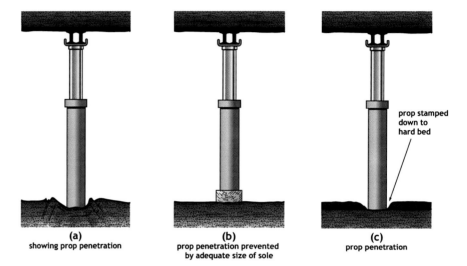

Figure 10:

Setting props, minimising prop penetration into the floor

(a)
showing prop penetration

(b)
prop penetration prevented
by adequate size of sole

(c)
prop penetration

162 If hydraulic props are being set under steel bars, they should either be fitted with friction caps or with heads that interlock with the roof bars. Where such caps or heads are not fitted, a wooden lid should be placed between the top of the prop and the underside of the bar.

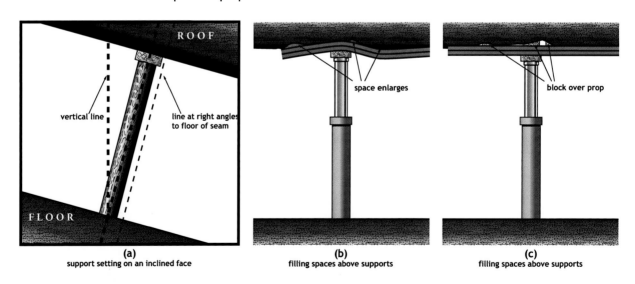

(a)
support setting on an inclined face

(b)
filling spaces above supports

(c)
filling spaces above supports

Figure 11:

Setting props in a variety of conditions

163 If there is a risk of hydraulic props springing out or falling, their tops should be effectively restrained by connecting a chain, wire sling or rope between the top of the prop and the bar.

is little to choose between two or more types or sizes of bars, managers should take other factors into account, such as ease of handling and setting, when they are deciding which is the best to use.

173 Corrugated bars are generally suitable only in situations where mining stresses are low and the roof is relatively strong. They are not rigid enough to be used in cantilever.

174 As a heading support, wooden bars are suitable only for narrow work where ground stresses are low. In most cases, wooden bars are not suitable for use as part of any face support system where they would have to be withdrawn and moved forward during each cycle. They are not very strong when set in cantilever and, in normal situations, should not be used above any prop that forms part of a prop-free-front face support system.

175 Only good quality wooden bars of reasonably consistent cross section should be used. Half-round or rectangular bars can be used, with their length varying according to the use to which they are to be put. Bars should be at least 125 mm wide and 60 mm deep.

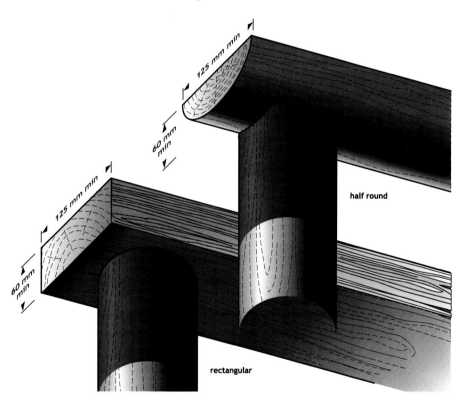

Figure 15:

Types of wooden bars

176 Wood bars are suitable for use in circumstances where part of the support system is sacrificed as part of the overall ground control measures; for instance, in areas where packs are being built, wood props and bars can be set initially and packed in. They can also be used in abnormal situations, such as supporting roof cavities.

Lids **177** If wood or steel props are set under steel bars, lids should be placed between the tops of the props and the underside of the bars. Lids help to ensure that the props are set tightly, and will prevent slip between the props and the bars.

178 If wood props are used, lids will help prevent bars from pushing into and splitting the tops of the props.

179 Lids are not needed above:

■ wood props greater than 0.2 m diameter;

■ wood props set under steel bars where the working height is less than 0.75 m;

■ props which are set to induce waste breaks;

■ props fitted with bar slide heads;

■ props fitted with friction caps;

■ steel props and steel bars that are coupled together.

180 If lids are used they should be at least 25 mm thick, and at least as wide as the diameter or width of the prop. The length of the lid should be at least twice the diameter or width of the prop.

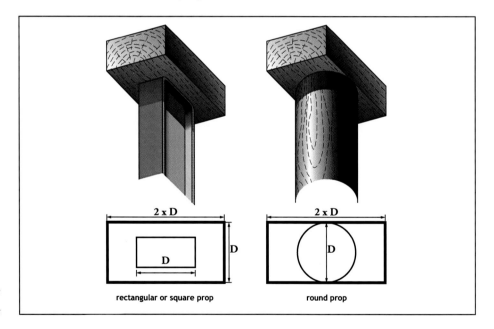

Figure 16: Minimum dimention of lids

181 A wood prop set under a wood bar need not have a lid, provided the prop is cut to the correct length to enable it to be set tightly.

Wedges **182** A wedge is a wedge-shaped piece of wood for tightening timber or steel props, or to tighten timber sets, against the roof and sides.

Nogs and sprags **183** A nog is a steel or wooden wedge inserted in the pre-cut face to prevent:

- coal spalling from the face;

- the formation of breaks in shot holes drilled into the face.

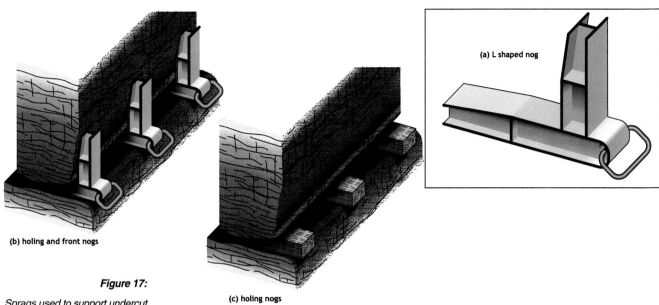

(a) L shaped nog

(b) holing and front nogs

(c) holing nogs

Figure 17:

Sprags used to support undercut

or middle cut coal face

184 Sprags, or stays, are another means of ground control and should be used where workers are at risk from overhanging coal spalling from the coal face.

(d) face sprags

Chocks or cribs

185 Chocks, or cribs, are useful in providing quick, strong support to reinforce weak or broken ground. They can be used on coal faces to provide a breaking-off line at the waste edge. Chocks can be used at face ends to provide support to ripping lips, face entrances and pack holes, and are used frequently in gate roadways to provide extra stability where necessary.

186 The load-bearing capacity of a chock depends partly on the manner in which it is set to floor and roof. Its strength will also vary according to its configuration and the type, quality and condition of material used. Its capacity and stiffness can be improved by increasing the contact area through the use of wider blocks or chock pieces, or by increasing the number of pieces in each layer.

187 Chocks forming part of a system of support should be built on a proper foundation and set tight to the roof.

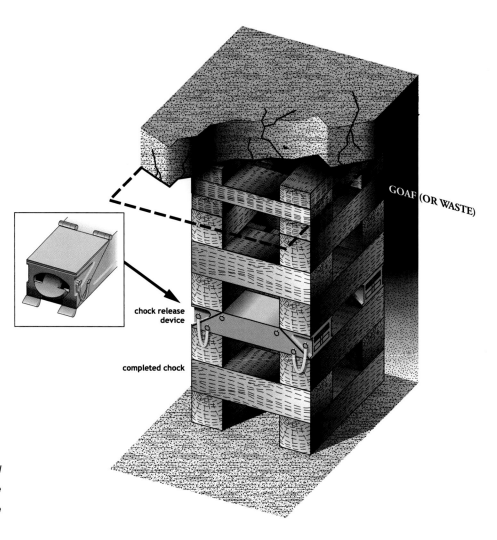

Figure 18: Wooden chock used as breaking off chock at the waste edge

188 When building a wood chock, it is important that the ends of the blocks in the layer above overlap the edges of the blocks in the layer below by at least 25 mm. This will delay the crushing of the ends of the blocks, so the chock will remain stable for a longer period.

189 The chock pieces should have flat bearing surfaces. Chock pieces are available with recesses cut into them so that they lock together to produce a strong, stiff and stable chock.

190 Every pack which is a permanent structure forming part of a system of support in a mine should, as far as possible, be made tight to the roof over its whole area.

191 Packs can be built along the sides of roads (gate side packs) to support the strata around the roadway, or at intervals along the line of a longwall face (strip packs) to control waste movement.

192 The size, number, type, position and method of construction of packs should be specified in the support rules.

193 Where packs form part of a face support system, the maximum width of roof exposed between packing cycles should not normally exceed 2.1 m (Schedule to regulation 8(3)).

Building packs by hand

194 Packs should be built in sections working safely from beneath supported ground. Support rules may specify the setting of props and bars as temporary support. Depending on the method of work adopted, these can either be packed-in or progressively withdrawn as sections are completed.

195 When building a debris pack by hand, the floor should be cleaned to provide a firm foundation for the pack walls. The pack walls should be thick

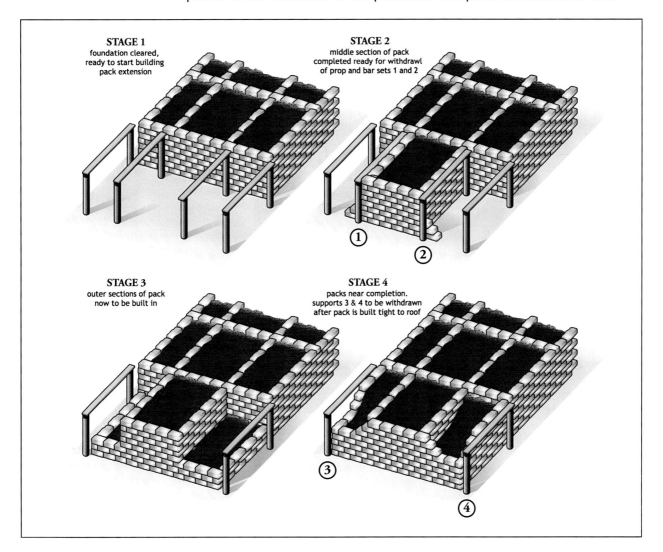

STAGE 1
foundation cleared,
ready to start building
pack extension

STAGE 2
middle section of pack
completed ready for withdrawl
of prop and bar sets 1 and 2

STAGE 3
outer sections of pack
now to be built in

STAGE 4
packs near completion.
supports 3 & 4 to be withdrawn
after pack is built tight to roof

Figure 19: Sectional method of packing

enough to support the pack, and where stones are used for the pack walls these need to be chosen to fit closely and firmly together with minimal gaps between them.

196 When nearing roof height, the debris should be rammed tight to the roof before completing the outer walls to ensure that the roof load is carried evenly over the whole pack width and not merely on the outer walls. The walls should taper slightly inwards towards the top of the pack.

Alternative packing systems

197 Packs can be built of debris, timber chocks, chocks filled with dirt and rubble, hessian or paper bags filled with dirt and rubble, aerated concrete blocks or similar lightweight aggregate blocks, or cement-based materials.

198 When timber chocks are used for packing, they should be set on a firm foundation and be made tight to the roof.

199 Aerated concrete blocks and lightweight aggregate blocks can be used to build roadside packs. Without reinforcement, packs built of these materials are liable to collapse under relatively small loads. It is important that the blocks are reinforced by wire mesh or other suitable materials, or that the void space in the middle is filled with pump-packing material.

Mechanised packing

200 Mechanised systems of packing can be used to speed up operations. Slusher buckets and monolithic pumped packs have been used in the UK for many years.

201 A slusher is an open-ended bucket, which collects debris from a pile (ripping lip etc) and drags the debris into the pack hole where the load is deposited. The operation is repeated until the pack is complete. A winch drawing ropes through a system of pulleys hauls the bucket.

202 Monolithic packs are formed by cement-based material pumped through a pipe, from a remote site, into a pack bag. The bag or a number of bags form the pack. The cement-based material has an inhibitor added to prevent premature setting of the material. Managers need to ensure that systems are in place to check that the properties of the placed material are within the design specification.

203 Many cement-based packing materials are either irritant or harmful in nature. If these materials are used, managers should take steps to ensure that workers mixing and using them are properly protected. Packing material manufacturers will give guidance on necessary precautions. These will include the use of risk assessment techniques to identify the steps to take to reduce exposure, such as the use of local exhaust ventilation and the provision of personal protective equipment, such as:

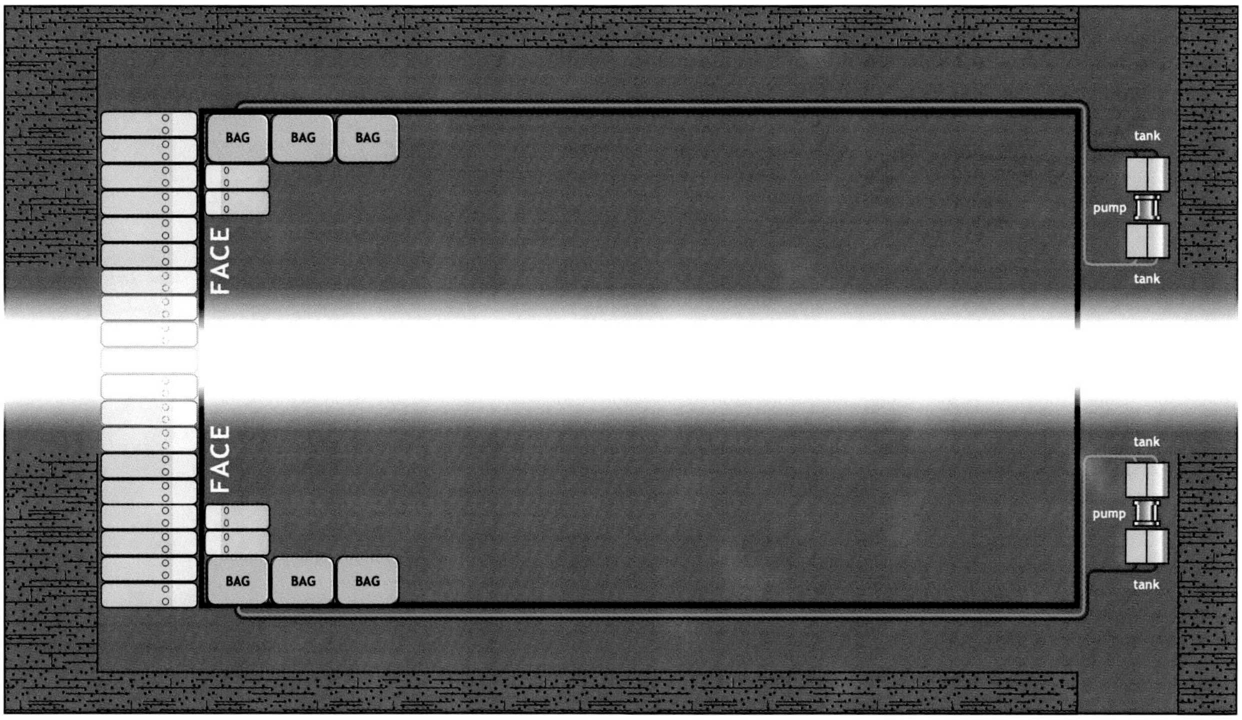

Figure 20: *Pump packing system*

■ eye protection;

■ dust masks;

■ gauntlets;

■ aprons.

Arches   **204** A wide variety of steel arches is available for support purposes.

Setting arches

205 Arch setting is a potentially hazardous operation, which gives rise to a number of risks to those workers setting it. The main hazards are falls of ground from the roof, face or sides and the handling of heavy objects.

206 Every arch girder which is set to support the roof or sides of any place should be set on a proper foundation and made tight to the roof and sides.

207 Making an arch tight to the roof and sides may involve packing in the space between the outer rim of the support and the roadway profile.

Struts   **208** Arches should be fastened to adjacent arches with ties or struts to secure and maintain their stability. Bolted ties or struts are much stronger than other types and will improve stability.

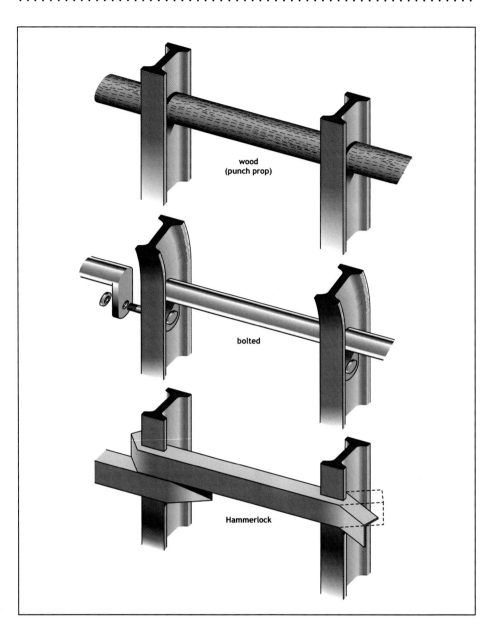

wood
(punch prop)

bolted

Hammerlock

Figure 21: *Types of strut*

Covering

209 Covering is used to prevent falls of roof or sides between supports.
The types of covering include:

■ steel mesh;

■ steel sheets;

■ punch props;

■ covering boards.

210 The space between the covering and the excavated profile needs to be
fully packed in to ensure an even distribution of load around the arch. This will
reduce the tendency for the arch to deform due to point loading.

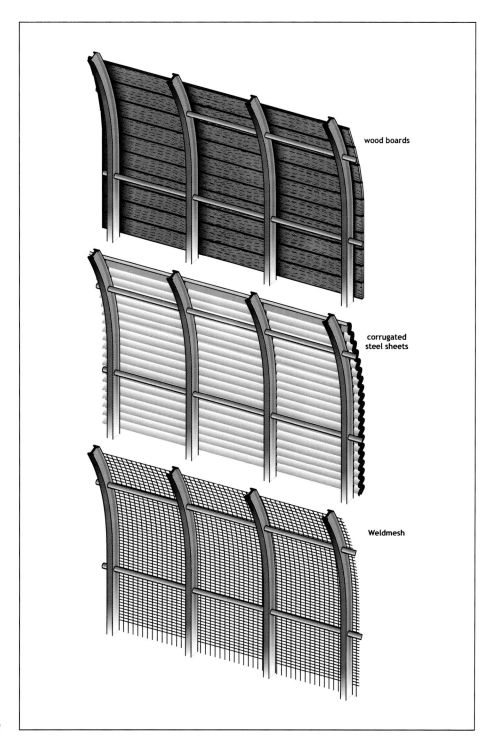

wood boards

corrugated
steel sheets

Weldmesh

Figure 22: Types of covering

Conventional setting

211 Conventionally set arches are usually erected using forepoles to support the crown piece until the legs or side members are erected.

212 Before starting to erect an arch, workers installing the supports should properly dress and scale the newly exposed ground, to ensure the removal of any loose material that might otherwise fall as the support is set. Managers should ensure that suitable scaling and dressing tools are readily available, so that workers can carry out this operation from a position of safety.

213 If ripping or heading machines are used, arch-lifting devices can be fitted to lift the arch crown piece and to hold it in place while the horseheads are advanced. In roadways or rippings advanced by the use of explosives, an arch-lifting bracket can be fitted to the front of the bucket of the mechanical loader.

214 Working platforms should be incorporated into most development/ripping machines to help in the installation of the crown or roof member. Other machines such as mechanical loaders can be modified to safely accept working platforms to help support installation.

215 If a working platform cannot be fitted to a machine, suitable scaffold platforms should be provided to allow people to work safely at height; for example, a platform may be based on girders attached by brackets, at about shoulder height, to the arch supports, along each side of the roadway. Girders spanning the width of the roadway between the two sides form the base of the platform, which will usually be wood scaffold boards.

216 There will be risks to people working close to exposed ground. While the risks from falls of roof may be apparent, many falls of ground accidents during arch setting are caused by falls from the face of the heading or ripping. These risks can be controlled by the proper use of temporary support, including protective devices. For example:

- In conventional rippings, L bars, supported by props and bars under the ripping, guard against falls from the face of the ripping.

- In both conventional rippings and in headings, forepoles support the crown piece while drop arms provide some protection from falls from the upper part of the face.

- Mechanical bolts, inserted into the exposed face, can be used to support wooden battens or mesh along the face of an exposed ripping or heading face.

- Side forepoles (or side poles) with battens pressed against the roadsides provide temporary support before installing the permanent support.

- Side shields do not support the roadsides but will deflect falls away from people working close to the face or ripping. There are several different types of side shield, ranging from prefabricated steel and mesh structures to pieces of conveyor belting hung from struts.

217 Managers should take care to ensure that workers can safely install and use the temporary support procedures they specify.

218 Temporary support arrangements need to take account of all stages in the support setting cycle, including packing around the arches.

219 In development roadways advanced by the use of explosives, the debris can effectively support the newly exposed face and sides. Therefore, only the minimum amount of debris should be excavated to allow the crown(s) to be set

. . . .

safely. Workers can then progressively excavate down the sides of the debris and set the legs. Temporary support will still be needed as the face and sides are progressively exposed.

Whole arch setting   220 Whole arch setting techniques have the potential to reduce risks to those setting support by reducing the amount of time they are exposed to potential falls of ground. Each arch is assembled a few metres back from the road head in a position where workers are not exposed to unsupported ground. Workers remain in a position of safety while the arch is lifted into position by the road header with a properly designed and tested arch lifting attachment.

221 Managers should specify in their support rules a safe system of work for whole arch setting following a suitable and sufficient assessment of risks for each site where the technique is being used. The system of work should include the procedures for:

■   clearing out for the arch legs;

■   strutting;

■   sheeting;

■   packing.

Strata reinforcement   222 Strata reinforcement can be used to supplement a primary support system where there is weak or broken ground. By stabilising and consolidating deforming strata, these techniques can:

■   reduce the number and severity of falls of roof or sides;

■   limit the rate and magnitude of ground deformation.

223 The strata reinforcement technique(s) chosen will depend on the condition of the strata, the method of work and the type of reinforcement needed to allow that work to be safely carried out. There are several methods of reinforcing strata:

■   dowelling with wooden or glass reinforced plastic dowels (GRP) using resin or cementitious grouts - usually applied where there may be a subsequent need to cut through the reinforcement (for example, on coal faces or at road heads);

■   grout injection, with or without dowels - usually applied to stabilise blocks of very weak or incompetent strat (for example, at fault areas);

■   sprayed lining (or shotcreting);

■   rock bolting and cable bolting - usually applied where strata is competent.

. . . .

Wood dowelling

224 Wood dowelling on coal faces can prevent coal spalling from the face and prevent the top of the seam parting from the strata above. This technique can therefore be used to prevent roof cavities forming in weak strata or to help regain control of the roof after a fall of ground.

GRP dowelling

225 There are a number of different GRP dowelling systems. Managers considering using them should ask the supplier(s) for more information.

Grout or resin injection dowelling

226 This system can be used to bind weak or broken ground prior to excavation. Managers thinking about using it should ask their supplier(s) for more information.

Sprayed linings

227 In the coal-mining sector, the application of sprayed cementitious linings is generally known as 'shotcreting'. Again, managers considering using sprayed linings should ask equipment and materials suppliers for specialist advice.

Bolting systems

228 Rock bolts, flexible bolts and cable bolts can be used to give extra support to a primary free standing support system. People using rock bolts and cable bolts in this way should refer to the relevant HSC guidance booklets (see references in Appendix 3).

Powered supports

229 The assessment of ground conditions made under regulation 5 will help to determine what type of powered support is best suited to the expected conditions or, if a particular type of powered support is already available, whether it can be used safely. The factors identified when making the assessment should be taken into account when preparing the coal face support design.

230 Managers should seek specialist advice, such as that provided by powered support manufacturers, if there is any doubt over powered supports' ability to perform safely in the environment where they are to be introduced

Beam tip to face distance

231 The designed distance between the tip of the powered support roof beam and the coal face before normal cutting should be kept to a practical minimum. In most circumstances the distance should not exceed 0.5 m (Schedule to regulation 8(3), paragraph 3(a)). If the designed distance is more than 0.5 m managers may have to notify HSE.

Figure 23: *Powered roof support*

Floor pressure

232 The maximum floor pressure that can be exerted by the powered supports should be compatible with the strength of the floor strata. Otherwise the bases of the powered supports could push into the floor and reduce the support available to the roof.

Setting and yield resistances

233 The designed yield and setting resistances of powered supports should be clearly specified in the design document. The designed setting resistance should be at least 75% of the designed yield resistance.

234 Details of the yield and setting pressures required to achieve the designed yield and setting resistances should be included in the support rules for that face. Operators, officials and members of the engineering staff need to know what the values are, so they can take action to identify and remedy any defects if the setting and yield pressures are lower than specified.

235 Workers, officials and members of the engineering staff should be encouraged to read the leg-circuit hydraulic pressure gauges, where fitted, as part of their normal duties.

236 Pressure gauges need to be kept clean and positioned where they can easily be read.

Powered support spacing

237 Modern powered supports are designed to operate with minimal distances between the canopies of adjacent supports and provide good protection from falls of ground between supports. Where older designs of powered supports are used, the distance between the edges of adjacent powered support canopies should be kept to a practical minimum to reduce the chance of debris falling between them while, at the same time, allowing powered supports to operate freely.

238 The design of some face-end support systems provides for two adjacent powered supports to be spaced some distance apart; for example, at face ends to cater for creep. In such circumstances other support needs to be set between these to properly control the roof; for example, pairs of steel bars supported by hydraulic props.

Powered support controls

239 All powered supports should have their operating controls and valves clearly labelled. Coal face workers, officials and maintenance personnel should keep the labels clean so they can be easily read.

240 Coal face workers and officials should be trained to use the type of powered supports that they are expected to operate.

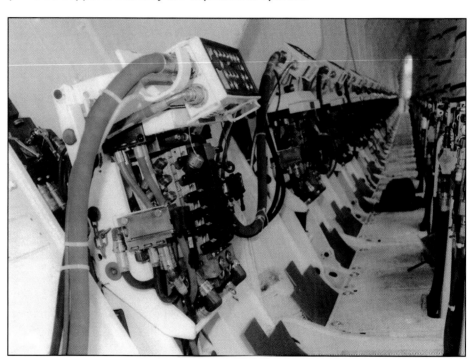

Figure 24: Powered support leg-circuit pressure gauges and readouts

241 If powered supports are fitted with advanced control features, such as adjacent control, automatic initiation or batch control etc, managers should take steps to ensure that people working on the coal face are trained to operate them. In particular, workers should understand the sequences in which the supports advance and be able to recognise the 'pre-movement' warning.

Advancing powered supports

242 To control the roof effectively and minimise the possibility of falls, powered supports should be advanced as soon as possible after the coal face-cutting machine has passed.

243 Sometimes the supports are designed to advance immediately after the coal face-cutting machine has passed, but before the AFC is advanced (a system known as 'immediate forward support' (IFS)). In this case, the supports should be advanced as close to the back of the coal-cutting machine as possible (Schedule to regulation 8(3), paragraph (c)).

244 If a coal face-cutting machine shears mineral deeper than 0.4 m, it should not normally come within 27 m of any powered support which has not been advanced from the previous cut (see Schedule to regulation 8(3), paragraph 3(b)).

Extension bars and face-sprags

245 Where extension bars are fitted to powered supports, they should be set as soon as is practicable after the coal face-cutting machine has passed.

246 Powered face sprags are recommended for all powered supports intended for use where the designed clearance between the top race of the AFC and the roof exceeds 2.3 m. Support rules should specify when and how they should be used.

Steep seams

247 Managers should ensure that powered supports for use on steep seam faces are designed and equipped for that purpose.

248 The sequence of advancing the supports, particularly those at the bottom of the face or at the bottom of each bank, should be included in the support rules.

Repair and maintenance

249 Each powered roof support should be separately represented within the manager's scheme for the systematic inspection, examination, testing, maintenance and repair of plant and equipment (see regulation 11(2) of the MASHAM Regulations 1993 and paragraphs 90-93 of the ACOP).

250 Power pack pumps and main feed and return lines should also be included within the scheme. The main hydraulic feed pressure and its flow rate should be monitored or checked frequently.

251 The composition and condition of the hydraulic fluid should be checked regularly. It should also be checked for any leakage.

252 If a support is damaged to the extent that its performance is impaired, the damaged part(s) should be repaired or replaced as soon as possible (see regulation 12(3)(a)).

253 If leg-circuit pressure gauges are fitted, they should be replaced as soon as practicable after damage or if they are not working.

254 Managers should ensure that operators, officials and those responsible for powered support maintenance are aware of the dangers of damaged high-pressure hydraulic hoses. These can lead to high-pressure fluid injection injuries.

Overhaul and modification of powered supports

255 After powered supports have been overhauled:

■ those which were approved under the Coal and Other Mines (Support) Regulations 1966 must continue to comply with the terms of the approval;

■ those that are 'CE' marked must continue to satisfy the essential safety requirements.

256 Modifications to:

■ canopies;

■ forepoling bars;

■ legs;

■ leg mountings;

■ control valves;

■ bases;

■ rams;

■ hydraulic circuits; and

■ any steep seam attachments

will affect the supports' performance and may be made only with reference to the original support design and relevant standard(s).

. . . .

GLOSSARY

Arch - two or more lengths of a rolled steel section joined together to provide support for the roof and sides of a roadway.

Bar - a support set parallel to the roof, usually on props or legs.

Chock/crib - A type of support usually formed from layers of hardwood chock pieces, concrete blocks, or steel girders.

Face working - means, in relation to a working face at which supports are systematically withdrawn, that part of the mine between the face and the front line of the packs, if any, or the last row of supports for the time being maintained, whichever is further from the face. In relation to a working face at which supports are not systematically withdrawn 'face working' means that part of the mine between the face and a line parallel to it and 3.7 m distance from it.

This is the legal definition from paragraph 7, Part I of the Schedule to regulation 8(3).

Foot block - a wood compression block placed between the floor and the bottom of a prop or leg.

Free standing support - a support which is set between the floor and roof eg arch, girder, other steel support, chock, prop and bar, powered support.

Ground control measure - a measure designed to control the movement of ground, including the provision and installation of support material (see regulation 2).

Hydraulic prop - an individual straight support set between the roof and floor, which is dependent on hydraulics for its setting and yield characteristics.

Lid - a wood compression piece, placed between a prop and a bar, or between a prop and the roof.

Member of the management structure - the mine manager or other person appointed to the mine management structure under regulation 10(1)(b) of the MASHAM Regulations.

Official of the mine - means a person appointed in the management structure in accordance with regulation 10(1)(b) of the MASHAM Regulations to thoroughly supervise persons in accordance with regulation 10(2)(a), or to perform inspections in accordance with regulation 12(2) of those Regulations.

Pack - a stone, cementitious or composite support built in the goaf and left there to resist strata movement.

. . . .

Powered support - a support which is advanced and set to the roof by mechanical energy, and uses an external power supply to provide the initial setting resistance.

Prop - an individual straight support member set between the roof and the floor.

Punch props - timber, batons or struts that fit into the flange of a steel support.

Worker - a person who sets or installs supports.

. . . .

APPENDIX 1 - MINIMUM STANDARDS FOR ALL TYPES OF SUPPORT SYSTEMS

<table>
<tr><td>Schedule to
regulation 8(3)</td><td>Part I
Support system standards</td></tr>
</table>

1   In the case of face workings where props are used -

(a)   the maximum distance between props in the same row shall be 1.2 metres;

(b)   the maximum distance between adjacent rows of props shall be 1.2 metres;

(c)   the sum of the distances between props in the same row and between adjacent rows of props shall not exceed 2.1 metres;

(d)   bars shall always be used above the props where the extracted height exceeds 0.6 metres; and

(e)   the maximum distance between the row of props closest to the face and the face shall be -

    (i)   where an armoured conveyor is used and persons do not normally work on the face side of the conveyor, 2 metres, and

    (ii)   in all other cases when filling or loading at the face has been completed, 0.9 metres.

2   In the case of face workings where bars are used -

(a)   the maximum distance between adjacent bars in the same row shall be 1.2 metres; and

(b)   bars should be advanced as soon as is practicable after extraction and set so that the maximum distance between the end of the bar closest to the face and the face shall be 0.4 metres.

3   In the case of face workings where powered supports are used -

(a)   such supports should be advanced as soon as is practicable after extraction and set so that the maximum distance between the end of the beam closest to the face and the face shall be 0.5 metres;

(b)   during normal production at any place where a machine is used which shears mineral to a depth exceeding 0.4 metres, the said machine must not be permitted to approach within 27 metres of any powered support which has not been advanced from the previous cut; and

. . . .

(c)   where an immediate forward support system is used, the supports shall be advanced -

    (i)   as close as practicable behind the coal getting machine, and

    (ii)   in any event, no more than 10 metres behind the coal getting machine.

4   For the purposes of paragraph 3 -

(a)   "powered support" means a support which is advanced and set to the roof by mechanical energy;

(b)   "beam" means that part of a powered support designed to be set to the roof;

(c)   "immediate forward support system" means a system of supports designed to be advanced and set to the roof immediately after extraction be a coal getting machine.

5   In the case of workings where packs are used -

(a)   the maximum width of roof exposed by the working of mineral since the completion of the last pack shall be 2.1 metres; and

(b)   the waste edge parallel to the face shall be no more than 1.5 metres in advance of the front line of pack bounding that waste.

6   In the case of face workings where persons work or pass more than 0.9 metres beyond the front row of props or other supports, temporary supports shall be used and no person may work more than 0.9 metres from a temporary support.

7   In this Part, "face working" in relation to a working face at which supports are systematically withdrawn, that part of the mine between the face and the front line of the packs, if any, or the last row of supports for the time being maintained, whichever is further from the face. In relation to a working face at which supports are not systematically withdrawn 'face working' means that part of the mine between the face and a line parallel to it and 3.7 m distance from it.

Part II
Support system standards for roadways

8   In the case of roadways where props and bars are used as the principal support -

(a)   the maximum distance between adjacent bars shall be 1.2 metres;

(b)   the minimum number of props per bar shall be 2; and

(c) the maximum distance from the last bar to the face shall be 3.5 metres.

9 In the case of roadways where steel arches are used as the principal support -

(a) the maximum distance between adjacent arches shall be 1.2 metres;

(b) the maximum distance from the last arch to the face shall be 3.5 metres.

10 In the case of roadways where rockbolts are used as the principal support -

(a) the minimum density of rockbolts in the roof shall be 1 bolt per square metre;

(b) the minimum length of rockbolts in the roof shall be 1.8 metres; and

(c) the maximum distance between the last completed row of rockbolts and the face shall be 3.5 metres.

11 In the case where machines are used to cut and simultaneously load, the maximum advance per cycle of any such machine shall be 1.2 metres.

12 In the case of roadways where persons work or pass in front of the last permanent support -

(a) temporary supports shall be used; and

(b) the maximum distance between the last permanent support and the first line of temporary supports shall be 1.2 metres, except where props are used, when that distance shall be 0.9 metres.

13 For the purposes of this Schedule "bar" means a support set between a prop and the roof.

APPENDIX 2 RELEVANT LEGISLATION

The Health and Safety at Work etc Act 1974

The Health and Safety at Work etc Act 1974 applies to all employers, employees and self-employed people. The Act protects not only people at work but also members of the public who may be affected by a work activity.

Self-employed staff

Although only the courts can give an authoritative interpretation of law, in considering the application of this guidance to people working under another's direction the following should be considered:

If people working under the control and direction of others are treated as self-employed for tax and national insurance purposes they are nevertheless treated as their employees for health and safety purposes. It may therefore be necessary to take appropriate action to protect them. If any doubt exists about who is responsible for the health and safety of a worker this could be clarified and included in the terms of a contract. However, remember, a legal duty under section 3 of the Health and Safety at Work Act (HSW Act) cannot be passed on by means of a contract and there will still be duties toward others under section 3 of the HSW Act. If such workers are employed on the basis that they are responsible for their own health and safety legal advice should be sought before doing so.

APPENDIX 3 - REFERENCES AND FURTHER INFORMATION

HSE publications

Guidance on the use of rockbolts to support roadways in coal mines HSE Books 1996 ISBN 0 7176 1082 9

Guidance on the use of cablebolts to support roadways in coal mines HSE Books 1996 ISBN 0 7176 1149 3

Guidance on the support of salvage faces in coal mines HSE Books 1997 ISBN 0 7176 1376 3

Supplementary guidance on the use of flexible bolts in reinforcement systems for coal mines HSE Books 2000 ISBN 0 7176 1861 7

Handbook on ground control at small mines CRR 264/2000 HSE Books 2000 ISBN 0 7176 1778 5

European and British Standards

BS 227:1995 *H-section steel arches for use in coal mines*

BS 7861:1999 *Strata reinforcement support system components for use in coalmines*

Part 1: *Specification for rock bolting*

Part 2: *Specification for cable bolting*

prEN 1804: *Machines for underground mines - Safety requirements for hydraulic powered roof supports*

Part 1 - *Support units*

Part 2 - *Power set legs and rams*

Part 3 - *Hydraulic control systems*

Part 4 - *Electro-hydraulic control systems*

Other documents

Specification of design factors and performance standards for adjustable props, prop ancillaries and roof bars 1985 (available from HSE Mines Inspectorate)

Specification of design factors and performance standards for a powered support - including cantilever bars and other ancillary equipment that may be fitted 1984 (available from HSE Mines Inspectorate)

Support of mine workings DTI 1973 ISBN 11 410164

. . . .

APPENDIX 4 HM INSPECTORATE OF MINES CONTACT DETAILS

National District office
HM Inspectorate of Mines
Health and Safety Executive
Edgar Allen House
241 Glossop Road
Sheffield
S10 2GW

Telephone: 0114 291 2390

Fax: 0114 291 2399